A Woman's Workshop
on
THE BEATITUDES
The Marks of a Christian

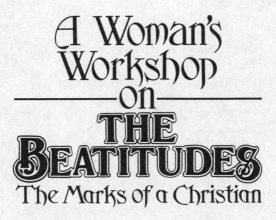

Books in this series—

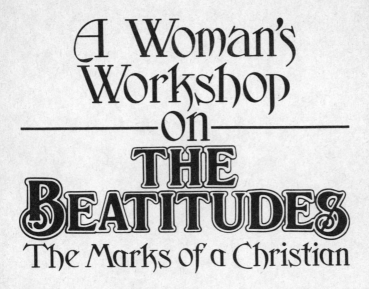

A Woman's Workshop on THE BEATITUDES

The Marks of a Christian

Student's Manual

Diane Brummel Bloem

ZONDERVAN PUBLISHING HOUSE OF THE ZONDERVAN CORPORATION GRAND RAPIDS, MICHIGAN 49506

A WOMAN'S WORKSHOP ON THE BEATITUDES — Student's Manual
Copyright © 1981 by The Zondervan Corporation
Grand Rapids, Michigan

ISBN 0-310-42651-0

Edited by Judith E. Markham and Linda DeVries

Printed in the United States of America

83 84 85 86 87 88 — 10 9 8 7 6 5 4 3

This book is lovingly dedicated to
my dear friend
THELMA PASTOOR BOONSTRA
who bears the marks of a Christian.

ACKNOWLEDGMENTS

I thank my husband, Robert C. Bloem, for studying these lessons with me, encouraging me, and helping me prepare this manuscript.

I thank the Reverend Leonard Greenway, Th.M., Th.D., for evaluating this manuscript, for encouraging me, and for offering his suggestions.

Most of all I thank the Lord for all He has taught me in this study. I pray that by His grace I may live all that I have learned.

PREFACE

Testing and *marks* are words that may arouse bad memories for some people. They sense again the tension and frustration of their school days: facing a page of questions, knowing that the mark they receive on the test will affect their future—either immediately when the report card goes home or in the future when they enter the work force. Test marks are considered indicators of intelligence, achievement, progress, or status.

Today many people enjoy testing themselves on all sorts of subjects by answering questions in magazines and then comparing their score with the chart at the end of the test. They "mark" or "grade" themselves.

But *mark* can mean more than a test score. God put a mark on Cain so that he could be easily identified (Gen. 4:15). In Revelation we read in many verses (13:16–17; 14:9, 11; 16:2; 19:20) about the "mark of the beast" which identifies those who serve Satan. Those who will live and reign with Christ are those who do not receive the mark of the beast but are easily identified as born-again Christians. Paul says wearily in Galatians 6:17, "From now on let no one make trouble for me, for I bear in my body the brandmarks of Jesus' owner-ship" (MLB). Anyone who examined Paul's life or saw the scars of persecution on his body could readily identify him as a Christian—belonging to Jesus.

7

In these lessons we will be testing and examining our hearts and lives to see if we can be easily identified as those who belong to Jesus (John 17:6–10, 24).

The first lesson introduces the background, the subject, and the setting and helps the students plan objectives. The last lesson encourages students to evaluate themselves and to plan how they can use what they have learned. Lessons 2 through 10 follow the pattern: Proclamation, Promise, Practice; in these lessons the students study Christ's challenging statement, examine the promises and how they motivate, and then are challenged to live what they learn.

For group study, all the questions should be answered in advance by the student; then the answers may be compared and discussed in the group meeting. If the lessons are used for personal study only, the questions should be answered by the student and then compared with the answers in the Leader's Manual.

Nothing I have studied has enriched my life and caused me to grow spiritually as much as the study of the Sermon on the Mount. It is my prayer that you will be blessed and challenged as I have been.

DIANE BRUMMEL BLOEM

LESSON 1

BIBLE PASSAGE

"Now when he saw the crowds, he went up on a mountainside and sat down. His disciples came to him, and he began to teach them. . . ."   Matthew 5:1–2

Before we begin to study Matthew 5:1–16, we should be alerted to several things. First, we should be aware that many of these verses contain paradoxes. A paradox is a statement that seems to be contradictory—something that common sense tells us is false, yet appears to be true. Do these statements make sense: "The poor are rich. Sad people are happy. Losers are winners"? These are some of the teachings of Jesus in the Beatitudes. When we look at them from Jesus' viewpoint rather than the world's, we will see that not only do these teachings make sense, but they give meaning and direction to all of life.

We should also be aware of the beautiful literary quality we find in these verses. Verses 3–10 are written in a form of Hebrew poetry called *synthetic parallelism* in which the second thought in each verse completes the first thought. Verses 13–16 are fine examples of using pictorial language to illustrate a spiritual truth. Many of the teachings in the Sermon on the Mount are given in proverb form; they contain distilled truth in an unforgettable form.

Jesus was the greatest teacher in the world. He used His ultimate creative skills to teach concepts in words people could easily understand and remember. We can see God's love for us expressed in the beautiful and efficient words He chooses as He teaches and communicates with us.

The knowledge that our great and mighty God cares so much for us and so desires to communicate with us that He adapts His speech to our needs should inspire us to praise Him as we begin this series of lessons.

1. Compare Matthew 5–7 with Luke 6:17–49. How are they alike? _____

   _____

   _____

   How do they differ? _____

   _____

   _____

2. Matthew 5–7 is generally called the Sermon on the Mount. A sermon may be defined as "a long, tiresome speech" or, more aptly, "an explication of a text of Scripture." Do you think this sermon was a long, tiresome speech? Why or why not? _____

   _____

   To what Word of God does this sermon point (John 1:1, 14)? _____

   _____

   _____

3. At what point in His ministry did Jesus speak these words? _____

_____

_____

4. To whom was this sermon given (Matt. 5:1–2; 7:28)?

_____

5. How does the world regard this sermon? _____

_____

_____

6. Matthew 5:3–11 is often referred to as the Beatitudes. What does *beatitude* mean? _____

_____

7. What does *blessed* mean? _____

8. Notice that verses 3–12 each contain a promise. Why does God give a promise with each beatitude?

_____

9. Is the promise a reward that is merited (Luke 17:10)?

_____

_____

10. Sometimes Matthew 5–7 is referred to as the Gospel of the Kingdom because the kingdom of heaven is mentioned several times (5:3, 10, 19–20). What is the kingdom of heaven? _____

_____

_____

_____

11. These lessons intensively study the identifying marks or characteristics of a Christian. Can an *unbeliever* exhibit all the characteristics pointed out in Matthew 5:3–16? Explain. _____

    _____

    _____

12. Will all these characteristics be found in every Christian?

    _____

13. Chapter 5 ends with these words: "Be perfect, therefore, as your heavenly Father is perfect." Does Jesus really expect us to be perfect? _____

    Is it possible for any human being to be perfect?

    _____

14. What do you hope to gain by studying these lessons?

    _____

    _____

LESSON 2

BIBLE PASSAGE

"Blessed are the poor in spirit,
for theirs is the kingdom of heaven."

Matthew 5:3

Sometimes the most difficult thing for us to do is to ask for help. Most of us know the joy of giving, but many of us have yet to learn the joy of receiving. Why is this? Perhaps we cannot bear to feel weak, helpless, or inadequate, so we work at projecting an image of strength and generosity. We are afraid to be vulnerable. We don't want to be beggars.

Saul (who later became the apostle Paul) felt strong as he set out for Damascus to persecute the Christians. Believing he had embarked on a righteous mission, he was equipped with self-confidence, health and strength, zeal, and letters— warrants and extradition papers—from the high priest. But the Lord stripped this all away in one moment. Gone was his self-righteousness; gone was his power; gone was his vision (Acts 9:1–9). Then the Lord became his strength and did wonderful things in and through him. Later Paul wrote to the Christians in Corinth, "For Christ's sake, I delight in weaknesses, in insults, in hardships, in persecutions, in difficulties. For when I am weak, then I am strong" (2 Cor. 12:10).

In this lesson we are challenged to admit our weakness, our total inadequacy. We are examining ourselves to find the first identifying mark of the citizens of the kingdom of heaven.

PROCLAMATION

1. What does it mean to be poor? _____

   _____

   _____

2. What *depth* of poverty is described in Matthew 18: 23–25? _____

   _____

   _____

3. What does it mean to be spiritually poor (Rev. 3:17; Rom. 3:23; Isa. 53:6; Rom. 6:23)? _____

   _____

   _____

   _____

4. How does it make you feel to know that you are spiritually bankrupt? Compare your feeling with Isaiah's in Isaiah 6:1–8, especially verse 5. _____

   _____

   _____

   _____

   _____

5. Can our good works be presented to God to earn our entrance to heaven (Hos. 12:8, 14; Gal. 3:10–11; Isa. 64:6)? _____

_____

_____

6. Then how can we come before God and hope to enter heaven (Titus 3:4–5; Eph. 2:8–9; Rom. 5:6–11)?

_____

_____

PROMISE

7. What is a kingdom? _____

_____

8. What powers does a king have? _____

_____

9. Who is the King of heaven and earth (Luke 19:37–40; John 18:36–37)? _____

10. What is required before we can enter the kingdom of heaven (Mark 1:15; John 3:3)? _____

_____

11. How do we receive this kingdom (Luke 12:32; Mark 10:15; Matt. 6:33)? _____

_____

_____

12. Is this promise fulfilled now, in the future, or both?

_____

PRACTICE

13. Why is it necessary to become poor in spirit before all the riches of the kingdom of heaven can be ours?

_____

_____

_____

14. Are poor people more likely to be poor in spirit?

_____

_____

15. Why do some dedicated church workers take vows of poverty? _____

_____

_____

_____

16. Does this beatitude teach that it is a blessing to be poor in material things? _____

_____

17. In what ways do you experience the triumph and power of the King and kingdom of heaven in your life? Consider Psalm 33:13–22; 2 Peter 2:9; Revelation 3:10; 17:14; 1 Corinthians 15:22, 54–58; 1 Peter 1:3–5.

_____

_____

_____

_____

LESSON 3

BIBLE PASSAGE

> *"Blessed are those who mourn,*
> *for they will be comforted."*
> Matthew 5:4

You have heard of people who laugh so hard they cry, or perhaps you yourself have cried tears of happiness. Children find this hard to understand. They say, "Why are you crying? I thought you were happy." Jesus presents this paradox to us: weepers are smilers; cry now so you can laugh; happy are those who mourn. In order to understand this, we must become as children and ask questions: Why are we mourning or crying? Why are we happy? How can this be? Let's look for the answers in this lesson.

PROCLAMATION

1. What does it mean to mourn? _____

_____

_____

2. How does the condition of being poor in spirit cause one to mourn (Rom. 7:21–25; Ps. 38)? _____

_____

_____

3. How is the grief caused by death of a loved one like the grief caused by our separation from God (Luke 16:26; Eph. 2:14)? _____

_____

_____

_____

4. What caused Jesus to weep at Lazarus's tomb and when He saw the city of Jerusalem (John 11:33–42; Luke 19:41–44)? _____

_____

_____

_____

PROMISE

5. In Isaiah 40:1–2, what are the words of comfort for God's people? _____

_____

_____

_____

6. How can the Holy Spirit comfort those who mourn because of their sins (John 14:26 KJV, ASV)? _____

_____

_____

_____

_____

7. It is a paradox to say that you will be happy (blessed) when you are mourning. How can you explain this?

_____

_____

_____

PRACTICE

8. Is mourning a necessary step before forgiveness is granted? _____

_____

_____

9. Should Christians always look like they are in mourning? Consider Matthew 9:15. _____

_____

_____

10. Does a Christian mourn only for his own sins?

_____

_____

11. How can Luke 6:25b and James 4:8–10 be used in evangelism? _____

_____

_____

12. What special comfort does this beatitude bring to Christians separated by death? _____

    _____

    _____

    _____

    _____

LESSON 4

BIBLE PASSAGE

> *"Blessed are the meek,*
> *for they will inherit the earth."*
>
> Matthew 5:5

A small child tugs at his mother's arm. He wants to tell her a secret and show her something. She stoops down to his level and tenderly puts her arm around him. That action defines meekness. The Hebrew word for meekness comes from a word meaning "to bend down," "to be low, depressed, or humble." The Greek word for meekness is often translated "gentle" (2 Cor. 10:1; Eph. 4:2; Col. 3:12). Just as the mother stoops down to the child's level, views things from his perspective, and gently places her arm around him, so the Lord Jesus Christ came down to earth, down to our level, and gently taught and healed people. Most important, He became obedient to the will of His Father.

PROCLAMATION

1. What do we mean by "meek"? Shy? Timid? Gentle? Weak? Humble? _____

   _____

   _____

2. If you feel inferior to others and lack self-confidence, does this mean you are one of the meek ones who will receive the promise in this beatitude? _____

   _____

3. Is *meek* the opposite of *proud*? _____

   _____

4. Is a person who is poor in spirit (bankrupt before God) and mourning because of his or her sins likely to feel proud and better than others? _____

   _____

5. The expression "meek as Moses" comes from Numbers 12:3. Read the following verses and try to discover why Moses is described as meek. Read Exodus 2:11–14; 3:6, 11; 4:1, 10–13, 29–31; 5:1, 22–23; 8:9; 10:28–29; 14:13–14, 31; 15:1–2; 17:2; 18:24–27; 32:19–22, 30; 33:12–23; Numbers 12:3, 7–8; 20:6–12.

   _____

   _____

   _____

6. Was Abraham meek (Gen. 13:8–12)? _____

7. What identifies Mary as a meek person (Luke 1:38)?

   _____

8. What qualities of meekness did Jesus display (Phil. 2:5–11; 1 Peter 2:21–25)? _____

_____

_____

9. What does Jesus teach about meekness in Matthew 18:1–5 and 20:26–28? _____

_____

PROMISE

10. What promise is given to the meek (Matt. 5:5)? See also Romans 8:12–17 and 2 Timothy 2:12. _____

_____

11. Is the promise of future reward (Luke 14:11) enough to encourage meekness? _____

12. What sustained the meek people listed in Hebrews 11? Note especially Hebrews 11:13–16, 39–40.

_____

13. Does the meek person receive any rewards in this life? If so, what are they (2 Cor. 6:10)? _____

_____

PRACTICE

14. Does a meek person make a good witness? _____

_____

_____

15. Should a Christian learn or practice self-assertion (defending oneself, speaking up, confronting people)? Explain. _____

    _____

    _____

16. If you are a leader and not a follower, does this mean you are not meek? _____

    _____

17. What makes a meek person brave (Eph. 6:10–18; Phil. 4:13)? _____

    _____

    _____

18. How can we learn to be meek (Matt. 11:28–29)?

    _____

    _____

LESSON 5

BIBLE PASSAGE

> *"Blessed are those who hunger and thirst*
> *for righteousness,*
> *for they will be filled."*
>
> *Matthew 5:6*

"What are you hungry for tonight?" I often ask my family as I frantically try to plan another supper. They never answer, "I'm really hungry for righteousness." If they did, I'd be shocked and would probably reprimand them for irreverence!

Jesus teaches us about a basic spiritual need by speaking of it as a basic physical need. This is an active beatitude. The person who is spiritually bankrupt, mourning for sins, and feeling meek now looks up for a way out. He or she *must* have righteousness. A great hunger and thirst arise in a starving, dehydrated soul.

PROCLAMATION

1. The Lord does not merely use the word *desire* here; He

speaks of hunger and thirst. Why did He choose these words? _____

_____

_____

_____

2. Have you ever been desperately hungry or thirsty? When? What effect did it have on your thoughts?

_____

_____

_____

_____

3. Psalm 42:1–2 compares the believer to a deer that has been running, chased by hunters, and is in need of water.

   a. What does the believer long for in these verses?

   _____

   b. What circumstances create this longing? _____

   _____

4. Suppose you had to explain the meaning of the word *righteousness* to a child or to someone with no religious background. What would you say? _____

_____

5. Whose righteousness do we need (1 Cor. 1:30)?

_____

6. What characteristics of a righteous life do you find in Ephesians 4:24 and Colossians 3:12? _____

_____

_____

7. Find three other Bible verses that give characteristics of the righteous life. _____

_____

_____

8. Read Matthew 22:1–14 (especially vv. 11–12) with Revelation 19:6–9 and 3:5. How necessary is this right-eousness? _____

_____

_____

9. Isaiah speaks much about the world's need of justice and righteousness. What do you learn about God's justice and righteousness in Isaiah 51:4–8? _____

_____

_____

_____

10. Is happiness or blessedness the *object* or *result* of this hunger and thirst for righteousness? _____

PROMISE

11. What assurance do we find in Isaiah 55:1–2?

_____

12. What does Jesus say He is in John 6:35? _____

_____

13. What does this mean to you? _____

_____

_____

14. Is this a once-in-a-lifetime or a continuous filling (John 4:14)? _____

_____

_____

15. What does Jesus mean in John 4:31–34? _____

_____

_____

16. How does being filled with the righteousness of Jesus in salvation create an ever-increasing appetite for righteousness (1 Peter 2:2–3)? _____

_____

_____

PRACTICE

17. How many hours of each day of your life are filled with planning meals, preparing food, eating food, and cleaning up after eating? _____

18. How does this compare with your time spent in planning, preparing, and partaking of spiritual food? _____

19. What impairs our spiritual appetite? _____

_____

_____

20. How can we find more time for spiritual nourishment?

_____

_____

_____

21. Are we less hungry for righteousness when we have plenty of physical food? _____

    _____

    _____

22. What creates spiritual hunger in your life? _____

    _____

23. What items in this week's news make you hunger and thirst for righteousness in your world? _____

    _____

    _____

24. How can you work for righteousness in your neighborhood, your schools, your family, and your community? _____

    _____

    _____

    _____

    _____

25. "Righteousness exalts a nation, but sin is a disgrace to any people" (Prov. 14:34). How can we work for righteousness in our nation? _____

    _____

    _____

    _____

LESSON 6

BIBLE PASSAGE

> *"Blessed are the merciful,*
>   *for they will be shown mercy."*
>   Matthew 5:7

Try to imagine the world without any acts of mercy—no hospitals, no missions, no charitable organizations, no child welfare programs, no courtesy, no kindness—the list goes on and on. Try to imagine your home devoid of mercy. Imagine bringing up your children and always giving them the justice they deserve, closing your ears and heart when they cry, "I'm sorry! I won't do it again!" How could we live in such an atmosphere?

Try to imagine yourself praying to God, asking for forgiveness because you "extended the truth," spoke hatefully to someone, or took some of God's honor for your own. Would you dare to ask forgiveness from the just God of the universe if you did not believe in His mercy?

Mercy is a divine attribute. It is Godlike. Humans only learn about mercy by experiencing it, by seeing God put His pity for us into action—doing something to rescue us from our helpless, sinful state. This beatitude may be read, "Blessed are the merciful, for they *have been shown* mercy." It is a two-way street: we receive mercy because we have been merciful; but we are merciful because we have received God's mercy.

In this beatitude we reach a turning point in our study. The saved sinner now looks beyond self and becomes aware of others. Eager to show thankfulness to God in every area of life, he or she passes God's mercy on to others.

PROCLAMATION

1. What is mercy? _____
   _____

2. What words do other Bible translations use for "mercy"? Compare Psalm 32:10 in various translations.
   _____
   _____

3. What is God's greatest act of mercy (Rom. 5:6-8)?
   _____

4. What gives a person the desire to show mercy (1 John 3:23)? _____
   _____

5. Why are we to show mercy (Titus 3:4-8; Eph. 4:32)?
   _____
   _____

6. To whom are we to show mercy (Luke 10:25-37)?
   _____

7. Does mercy go beyond an expression of sympathy (James 2:14–17; 1 John 3:17–18)? _____

   _____

8. What can we learn from the parable of the unmerciful servant (Matt. 18:21–35)? _____

   _____

   _____

PROMISE

9. Why do the merciful need mercy (Matt. 6:14–15)?

   _____

   _____

10. When will they receive mercy (Ps. 23:6)? _____

    _____

11. How did Onesiphorus show mercy (2 Tim. 1:16–17)?

    _____

    _____

12. How was he to be rewarded (2 Tim. 1:18)? _____

    _____

13. Job reminded God that he had been merciful (Job 31:16–23). Did God respond by showing Job mercy (Job 42:1–6, 10)? _____

    _____

    _____

    _____

PRACTICE

14. Should Christians show mercy only to Christians? Explain the implications of Matthew 9:10–13 and Galatians 6:10. _____

_____

_____

15. Should the church give financial aid if needy members are eligible for public assistance? _____

_____

_____

16. Are we expecting the government to fulfill our responsibility to show mercy? _____

_____

17. Are you showing mercy when you pay taxes, knowing that some of the money will be used for welfare programs? Explain. _____

_____

_____

18. Is a clean, attractive, polite person more likely to receive mercy than a repulsive person? Consider James 2:1–9.

_____

19. Is a clean, attractive, polite person more *deserving* of mercy than a repulsive person? _____

_____

20. Must acts of mercy always be accompanied by proclamation of the Word of God? _____

_____

LESSON 7

BIBLE PASSAGE

"Blessed are the pure in heart,
for they will see God."

Matthew 5:8

Have you ever noticed how many television commercials deal with cleanliness—clean clothes, clean floors, clean bathrooms, clean dishes, clean hair, clean teeth, clean air? The civilized world is obsessed with external cleansing.

Have you ever noticed how many television programs deal with sin—murder, rape, adultery, robbery, child abuse, blackmail, assault, drug abuse, drunkenness? The "civilized" world seems to crave a mental diet of filth.

I am reminded of Jesus' words: "Woe to you, teachers of the law and Pharisees, you hypocrites! You clean the outside of the cup and dish, but inside they are full of greed and self-indulgence. Blind Pharisee! First clean the inside of the cup and dish, and then the outside will also be clean" (Matt. 23:25–26).

This lesson deals with inner cleanliness—pure hearts. How do we get them? Why should we want them? What difference will they make in our lives?

PROCLAMATION

1. What examples can you give of the Bible's use of the word *heart*? (Your concordance will help you.)

   _____

   _____

   _____

2. What does *heart* mean in our text? _____

   _____

   _____

   _____

3. What does *pure* mean? _____

   _____

   _____

   _____

4. What does James mean when he speaks of the condition of double-mindedness that necessitates our purification (James 4:8)? _____

   _____

   _____

   _____

5. How are believers double-minded today? _____

   _____

   _____

   _____

6. Contrast this state of mind with that described in Acts 2:46 and Ephesians 6:5–8. Note that the word translated "sincere" in the NIV is translated "singleness" in the KJV.

_____

_____

_____

7. How do our hearts become pure (Ps. 51)? _____

_____

_____

_____

8. What other Bible verses use the metaphor of washing for cleansing from sin? _____

_____

_____

_____

9. How does 1 John 3:2–3 relate to this beatitude and give us hope and challenge? _____

_____

_____

_____

PROMISE

10. What do John 1:18; 6:46; 14:9; and 1 Timothy 6:16 say about seeing God? _____

_____

_____

_____

_____

_____

11. What danger was there in seeing God (Exod. 33:20–23)?

_____

_____

12. Isaiah saw a vision of God (Isa. 6:5). How was he able to live through this experience (6:7)? _____

_____

_____

13. Why is it a blessing to see God? _____

_____

14. When will the pure in heart see God (1 John 4:12; Rev. 1:7; 22:4)? _____

_____

_____

PRACTICE

15. How will the Christian's life differ from the unbeliever's life (Heb. 12:14; 1 Peter 4:1–5; 3 John 11)? _____

_____

_____

_____

16. How can Philippians 4:8 help us to be pure in heart?

_____

_____

_____

17. Should Christians keep themselves from all contact with evil or evil, uncleansed persons? For example, should they read newspapers or books which tell of evil? Should they visit jails or associate with co-workers who are unsaved? _____

_____

_____

_____

18. Read Psalm 139:23–24. Why can a Christian say this with confidence? _____

_____

_____

LESSON 8

BIBLE PASSAGE

*"Blessed are the peacemakers,
for they will be called sons of God."*

Matthew 5:9

"You're just like your mother," a woman told me. I stopped to think about my mother and what she was like. What did the woman see in me that was like my mother? Surely she wasn't speaking of my looks, though I do have some features like my mother. She must have been referring to my nature, my behavior or perhaps my value system.

Even adopted children are often told that they resemble their parents. Sometimes they do, but more often they resemble their adoptive parents in lifestyle and attitudes.

In this beatitude we are promised that if we are peacemakers, we will be called sons (children) of God. We are the adopted children of the One who so wanted peace in His family that He paid the supreme price for reconciliation. He restored the fellowship of God and man. When we work for peace, people will say, "You're just like your Father!"

PROCLAMATION

1. What is peace? _____

   _____

2. What kind of peace is referred to in 2 Kings 20:19 and Psalm 122:6–9? _____

   _____

3. What kind of peace is referred to in Isaiah 26:3; John 14:27; and Romans 8:6; 15:13? _____

   _____

4. Why does God call us to live in peace (1 Cor. 7:15)?

   _____

   _____

5. Who is the greatest peacemaker? Read Ephesians 2:13–18. _____

   _____

6. How did He make peace (Eph. 2:13; Rom. 5:1)?

   _____

   _____

7. Are the peacemakers referred to in Matthew 5:9 to make peace in all situations—spiritual and political?

   _____

8. Since all Christians are called to live at peace and be peacemakers, what personal qualities enable us to make peace? See James 1:19 and 1 Corinthians 13:4–7.

   _____

   _____

PROMISE

9. Why are peacemakers called the children of God?

   _____

   _____

10. How does this promise motivate you to be a peace-
    maker? _____

    _____

    _____

PRACTICE

11. Which is easier—to make peace between others or be-
    tween yourself and another? Why? _____

    _____

    _____

    _____

12. Can you share any blessed experiences of peacemaking?

    _____

    _____

    _____

13. How can a lack of peace in the home or congregation
    have an adverse effect on a Christian's peacemaking ef-
    forts? _____

    _____

    _____

14. What advice for peacemaking is given in Romans 12:17–20? _____

    _____

    _____

    _____

15. Should we look for opportunities to act as peacemakers?

    _____

    _____

    _____

16. How can you make peace between quarreling children?

    _____

    _____

    _____

17. Does the Bible call us to be pacifists—nonparticipants in war? _____

    _____

    _____

    _____

18. Are we to work for peace at any price? _____

    _____

    _____

19. How is a missionary a peacemaker? _____

    _____

    _____

    _____

20. What are we promised in James 3:18? What does this mean? _____

_____

_____

_____

_____

LESSON 9

BIBLE PASSAGE

*"Blessed are those who are persecuted
because of righteousness,
for theirs is the kingdom of heaven."*

Matthew 5:10

Persecution for righteousness' sake began just a few years after the creation of humanity. Cain killed Abel because the Lord approved of Abel. In this last beatitude, Jesus announces that those who are persecuted for righteousness will be happy, joyful, and filled with a sense of spiritual well-being. But how can that be? Abel died! And throughout the centuries thousands have suffered and died because of their faith in Christ and their service for Him.

This lesson introduces the study of persecution as a mark of a Christian. Is it necessary to suffer persecution to be identified as a Christian? What is the cost of becoming a disciple of Christ? Is it worth it? These matters will be discussed in this lesson.

PROCLAMATION

1. What is persecution? _____

   _____

2. Christ was perfectly righteous. Was He persecuted (John
   15:18–20; 1 Peter 2:21–24)? _____

   _____

3. If we are Christlike, will we be persecuted (2 Tim. 3:12;
   Phil. 1:29)? _____

   _____

4. Why is persecution to be expected by righteous people
   (John 15:21–22)? _____

   _____

   _____

5. Who does the persecuting (John 1:11; 11:57; 2 Cor.
   6:3–13)? _____

   _____

   _____

6. Can you think of any Bible characters who were persecuted for righteousness' sake? _____

   _____

PROMISE

7. Why is the same promise given in verse 10 as in verse 3?

   _____

   _____

8. How does this promise comfort those who are undergoing persecution? _____

_____

_____

_____

9. Does this blessing come to those who are persecuted for any cause: e.g., for equal rights, gun control laws, recreational privileges, political activities (1 Peter 4:14)?

_____

_____

_____

_____

PRACTICE

10. Are peacemakers and merciful people ever persecuted because of their helpful activities? _____

_____

_____

11. What forms does persecution for righteousness take in the free world today? _____

_____

_____

12. How should a Christian face persecution (1 Peter 3:8–9; 4:19)? _____

_____

_____

13. How did Paul and Silas respond to persecution (Acts 16:22–25)? _____

_____

_____

14. Should we feel persecuted for righteousness if we have been offensive or rude in witnessing for Christ (1 Peter 3:15–16)? _____

_____

_____

15. Jesus was persecuted by the religious leaders and people of His day. Do we as church members ever persecute others because of their righteousness? _____

_____

_____

_____

16. If your business position would be seriously threatened unless you urged someone to make an unwise purchase, or falsified a report, or lied for your employer, would this constitute persecution for righteousness' sake?

_____

_____

17. Should we avoid telling new Christians about the "cost" of belonging to Christ? Will it discourage them (Luke 14:25–33; Matt. 10:38; 16:24)? _____

_____

_____

_____

18. How does the Lord strengthen and sustain His suffering, persecuted people (Luke 21:12–19; Matt. 28:20b; Heb. 13:6)? _____

_____

_____

_____

_____

_____

LESSON 10

BIBLE PASSAGE

> *"Blessed are you when people insult you,*
> *persecute you and falsely say all kinds*
> *of evil against you because of me.*
> *Rejoice and be glad, because great is your*
> *reward in heaven, for in the same way*
> *they persecuted the prophets who were*
> *before you."*
>
> *Matthew 5:11–12*

"Sticks and stones may break my bones, but words can never hurt me," we chanted as children and then went home to cry because our spirits were crushed.

As Jesus points out in these verses, words are powerful weapons. Jesus' own words were twisted and used to convict and kill Him (Matt. 26:63–66; John 18:33–38; 19:12–16). Many of His followers have suffered and died because of words launched by tongue or pen. But the Word of God is an invincible weapon given to Christians to use in times of persecution—for their comfort and for their defense (Eph. 6:17).

PROCLAMATION

1. How does verse 11 differ from verse 10? _____

_____

2. Does this blessing extend to anyone who is insulted or falsely accused (1 Peter 4:14–16)? _____

_____

3. Is there room for self-pity if we are persecuted for right-eousness' sake? In other words, should we enjoy being martyrs? _____

_____

_____

4. Should we, as Christians, wish others to speak well of us (Luke 6:26)? _____

_____

5. Can you name some Old Testament prophets who were persecuted? _____

_____

_____

6. Why were the prophets persecuted? _____

_____

_____

PROMISE

7. Give at least two reasons why a Christian can find joy in persecution. Consider 2 Corinthians 4:17–18; 1 Peter 4:13, 16; 1 John 2:5–6 with John 15:18–20.

_____

_____

_____

_____

8. What joy helped Jesus bear persecution (Heb. 12:2)?

_____

_____

9. How does the promise of a reward in heaven help us bear the suffering? _____

_____

_____

10. Does a Christian's suffering for righteousness' sake *earn* the reward for him or her? _____

_____

_____

PRACTICE

11. Should a Christian ever resist persecution (1 Peter 2:21–23)? _____

12. If you lose your job because you won't work on Sunday or won't lie for your employer, should you sue to get your job back? _____

_____

_____

_____

13. Is persecution good for the church? _____

_____

_____

_____

14. Should Christians court persecution or hope to be persecuted for righteousness' sake? _____

_____

_____

15. Should the lack of open or physical persecution be regarded as a blessing? _____

_____

16. Is the lack of persecution an indication that one is not living the Christian life? _____

_____

17. What comfort do you find in 1 Peter 5:10?

_____

LESSON 11

BIBLE PASSAGE

"You are the salt of the earth. But if the salt loses its saltiness, how can it be made salty again? It is no longer good for anything, except to be thrown out and trampled by men."

Matthew 5:13

Along with the eight Beatitudes, there are two more marks of a Christian found in Matthew 5. Jesus teaches us how to live thankful, effective Christian lives by using, as examples, salt and light. In this lesson we will consider the first.

Everyone uses salt. Salt is so common that we take it for granted. Jesus calls His people "the salt of the earth." He is not speaking to famous, talented, "spicy" people. He is speaking to all the common, seemingly insignificant people—Christians—who are called to penetrate the world with Christianity, to preserve the world, and to flavor life.

1. What would the world be like if there were no living, practicing Christians in it? _____

_____

_____

2. What specific things can Christians, as salt, do to keep the world from becoming utterly decadent? _____

_____

_____

_____

3. What use for salt is mentioned in Job 6:6? _____

_____

4. Describe a Christian who is like salt without taste.

_____

_____

5. Read Colossians 4:6. Repeat this verse in your own words and explain why salt is used as an example here.

_____

_____

_____

6. Why was salt used on a newborn baby as mentioned in Ezekiel 16:4? How can a Christian, as salt, be used in this way? _____

_____

_____

_____

7. List at least three more uses for salt and tell how they can explain the Christian's role in the world. For example: Salt makes us thirsty so that we will drink and keep a healthy amount of water in our bodies. A Christian will live so that others will thirst for Christ, the water of life, whom we must have for eternal life.

_____

_____

_____

_____

_____

_____

_____

8. Is too much salt as bad as too little salt? Can Christians "come on too strong" and therefore kill the tender plant that springs up when the Word is heard (Judg. 9:45; Ps. 107:33–34)? _____

_____

_____

9. Does salt do any good while it stays in the shaker on the shelf? What must be done with salt for it to be effective?

_____

_____

10. Why would Christians be inclined to live in a church-controlled environment or an isolated Christian-oriented community? _____

_____

_____

11. In John 17:6–19 Jesus speaks of His disciples as being in the world, but not of the world. Explain this.

_____

_____

12. In 2 Corinthians 6:17 Christians are told to be separate. Should Christians, as salt, separate themselves from the world? If so, when? _____

_____

_____

13. How did Jesus practice both of these truths; that is, the need to be salt in the world but also to be separate (Matt. 9:9–13; 11:19; 14:23; Mark 6:30–34)? _____

_____

_____

14. Citizens of the kingdom of heaven are to be pure in heart (Matt. 5:8). If they permeate the world as salt, isn't there a danger that they will be contaminated and lose that purity? _____

_____

_____

15. Should Christians have their own social organizations or join those of the world? _____

_____

16. Should Christians attend business parties where there is drinking and/or worldly entertainment? _____

_____

17. How does Jesus regard Christians who are unwilling to live the Christian life in the world (Matt. 5:13)?

_____

18. How can a Christian become "resalted" (John 15:7–8)?

_____

_____

LESSON 12

BIBLE PASSAGE

"You are the light of the world. A city on a hill cannot be hidden. Neither do people light a lamp and put it under a bowl. Instead they put it on its stand, and it gives light to everyone in the house. In the same way, let your light shine before men, that they may see your good deeds and praise your Father in heaven." Matthew 5:14–16

The children carried flashlight candles and squirmed with excitement at the Sunday school program. They couldn't wait to sing, "This little light of mine, I'm going to let it shine." They especially liked to cover their lights and sing, "Hide it under a bushel, NO!" But the best part (and the most difficult to coordinate) was flicking the light off and on again during the stanza, "Won't let Satan blow it out; I'm going to let it shine."

This well-loved children's song is based in part on the verses we study in this lesson. Jesus speaks to us as to children, patiently illustrating the truth that Christians must be visible lights, bringing love and hope and joy so that all who see them in action will say, "God is great!"

1. If Jesus is the Light of the World (John 8:12), how can Christians also be the light of the world (Matt. 5:14)?

   _____

   _____

2. What is the source of the Christian's light (Ps. 18:28)?

   _____

   _____

3. What do these verses tell us (Ps. 84:11; Mal. 4:2; Matt. 17:2; Rev. 21:23)? _____

   _____

4. How is a Christian like the moon? _____

   _____

5. History speaks of the Age of Enlightenment and the Dark Ages. Is it correct to say that the unsaved world seeks its light from science, education, and the like? _____

   _____

6. Why do cities practice blackouts in wartime? _____

   _____

   _____

7. Why do Christians sometimes hide their light—hide the fact that they are Christians? _____

   _____

   _____

8. Why is much crime perpetrated at night? _____

   _____

   _____

9. What does Psalm 139:11–12 teach us about this?

_____

_____

10. How do you feel about your housekeeping effectiveness on a brilliant, sunny day? _____

_____

11. What is referred to as light in Psalm 119:105, 130 and 2 Corinthians 4:6? _____

_____

12. How is that light related to Christ as the Light (John 1:1–5)? _____

_____

_____

13. How does the Bible help Christians shine for the Lord?

_____

_____

14. How does light help things grow? Apply this to the Christian's life. _____

_____

15. How does light reveal beauty? Consider Genesis 1:1–5. How can beauty be truly appreciated only in the light of Christ? _____

_____

_____

_____

_____

16. How do unbelievers benefit from the light cast by Christians? _____

_____

_____

_____

17. Why is the light of living, practicing Christians resented by the world (John 3:19–21)? _____

_____

_____

18. What specific things can you do as the light of the world (Matt. 5:16)? _____

_____

_____

_____

19. Is Matthew 5:16 a request or a command? _____

20. What is the purpose of the Christian's good works (Matt. 5:16; 1 Peter 2:9)? _____

_____

LESSON 13

SUMMARY

Testing time is here. After studying these lessons, it is time for us to look at our lives and see if we bear the marks of a Christian. It is time for us to ask how we can use what we have learned and if our lives will be noticeably changed by these words of Jesus.

This is not the final examination. That will come on Judgment Day when Jesus opens the record books. May He find our names in His book with the notations: Redeemed. Course completed. Promoted to glory.

1. Why is it good for people to study the Beatitudes?

    _____

    _____

    _____

2. What have you gained by studying these lessons? Compare your answer to this question with your answer to question 14, Lesson 1. _____

    _____

_____

_____

_____

3. Compare the rewards and promises in Matthew 5:3–12 with the immediate gratification demanded and expected by most people in Western cultures today. See also Hebrews 11:13–16, 24–28, 39–40. _____

_____

_____

_____

4. Everyone seems to be "pursuing happiness." Do the verses studied in these lessons contain the answer to how to obtain it? Explain. _____

_____

_____

5. How could you use Matthew 5:3–6, 48 to present the need for the Savior? _____

_____

_____

_____

6. How could you use Matthew 5:7–16 to help a new Christian understand how to live for Christ and what to expect as a response from the world? _____

_____

_____

_____

_____

7. How can believers be sure they will receive the rewards promised in these verses (Num. 23:19; Josh. 21:45; 23:14; 1 Kings 8:56; Heb. 6:16–19a; 10:23–24)?

_____

_____

_____

8. Are all of these marks of a Christian present to some extent in your life? (Answer privately and personally.)

_____

_____

9. Can others readily identify you as a Christian because they see these characteristics in you? (Answer privately and personally.) _____

_____

10. How can we help one another grow stronger as citizens of the kingdom of heaven (Luke 4:4; 11:28; 1 John 4:7–21; 1 Peter 3:8–17; Eph. 6:10–18; Heb. 10:24–25)? _____

_____

_____

_____

_____

_____